# CLARITY IS POWER

“Clarity is Power" book series, is a collection of wisdom from thought-provoking Q and A with renowned Mahatria. His unique gift of answering questions spontaneously is captured in this book, offering life-changing insights.

The "Clarity is Power" series comprises 11 illuminating volumes, each addressing essential aspects of life:

1. Attitudes
2. Self-Discipline
3. Emotional Development
4. Relationships
5. Marriage
6. Parenting
7. Student Life
8. Career Growth
9. Leadership and Entrepreneurship
10. Spirituality
11. Faith



**Mahatria** Spiritualist | Thought leader | Diviner of infinitheism

For nearly three decades, Mahatria has empowered millions worldwide to achieve holistic abundance. His profound wisdom uplifts people in health, wealth, love, bliss, and spirituality.

infinitheism, the path divined by Mahatria, inspires breakthroughs for anyone who ardently desires abundance by transforming the human spirit to have faith in its infinite potential.

*First published in India*

**Manjul Publishing House**

• 2nd Floor, Usha Preet Complex,
42 Malviya Nagar, Bhopal 462 003 - India
• C-16, Sector 3, Noida, Uttar Pradesh 201301 – India
Website: www.manjulindia.com

*Distribution Centres:*
Ahmedabad, Bengaluru, Bhopal, Kolkata, Chennai,
Hyderabad, Mumbai, New Delhi, Pune

In association with:

infinitheism

3, 3rd Cross Road, R A Puram,
Chennai, Tamil Nadu, India
www.infinitheism.com

**FAITH** (CLARITY IS POWER)

by

This edition first published in 2016
Third impression 2024

ISBN 978-93-5543-434-0

Printed and bound in India by Thomson Press (India) Ltd.

# FAITH

mahātria

# CONTENTS

# CONTENTS

# 1

*I want to surrender, but I want to intellectually satisfy myself before I surrender. People say that if you use your intelligence, then it is not surrender. How can you surrender without understanding what you are doing?*

Without a questioning intelligence, materialistic progress is not possible. With a questioning intelligence, spiritual progress is not possible. Use your intelligence to progress in the without, but subordinate that very intelligence for progress in the within. Arjuna too kept asking questions. However, though Arjuna's questions were to Krishna, he never questioned Krishna. Ask questions to the Master. Don't question the Master.

A father and his son had to cross the road. The traffic was heavy. The father stretched out his hand and asked his son to hold on to a finger. The father took two steps forward and the son too moved forward. Then he moved a little to the side, and so did the son. Then the father ran five steps forward, and the son ran along. The father was then forced to go back a few steps, and the son did so too. Finally, they crossed the road. In this entire process of crossing the road, the responsibility of making the right decisions was with the father. What was it to the son - just a game of surrender! He trusted the finger he was holding on to and everything else happened. He didn't have to carry the burden of responsibility; instead, he enjoyed the freedom of surrender. If his intelligence had interfered with the intelligence of the hand that was leading him, crossing the road would have been a miserable process, not a peaceful one.

In fact, the very essence of surrender is transference of responsibility. Surrender is to know - it is not my will, but thy will that will be done. Surrender is about finding that finger to which you subordinate your intelligence. I can understand your apprehension - How can I trust someone in a world of so many spiritual frauds?

Fortunately, surrender is not a decision. It is a happening. Keep the seeker in you alive. Seek with all your heart. Let there be devotion in your seeking. When you are ready, your teacher will appear. A Master-seeker relationship is not a matter of judgement. It is a matter of chemistry. It is a spontaneous reaction. You will lose yourself to that very presence. The drop of water, in dropping into the ocean and merging with the ocean, loses its individual identity, but becomes the ocean in the process. Surrender is the subordination of Arjuna's intelligence so that Krishna's intelligence can pave the way. Surrender isn't a give up. It is a go up.

When you find that presence in which surrender can happen, a question on surrender, or a question on how to surrender will no longer arise in your mind. It will all happen. From then on, that presence will prevail in you, around you and will always be with you. ●

***Surrender is about finding that finger to which you subordinate your intelligence.***

mahātria

2

*What will be the
right time
for meditation?*

Suppose I tell you it is four o' clock in the morning you won't meditate at all! But it is said that *Brahma muhurth* which is around four a.m. is the most ideal time for meditation. A lot of these things were created at a time when we didn't have artificial lighting. So, in the yesteryears, people generally rose by sunrise and retired after sunset. They slowly wound up their day as the sun moved towards the west, since they didn't have any external sources of entertainment. But now, the situation is different and hence we have embraced a lot of lifestyle changes in the last few centuries.

Everything has evolved over time; we do not eat or dress the same way as we did thousands of years back. The way we communicate, the way we do business, the way we earn a living, the way we elect a government, the way we entertain ourselves, the way we listen to music, the way we commute from one place to the other - everything has changed. There is only one thing that has not evolved and that is religion and religious practices. They still remain the same as prescribed a few centuries back.

I am not saying truth changes with time, but the application changes. No messiah, no prophet came and gave you a new truth; truth is timeless, it has always been... According to the temperament of people the same truth had to be contemporized differently on its application, i.e., methodology on how to apply in daily life. Time and again rishis and yogis did this and created a new version of the existing truth.

What is religion? Religion is nothing but contemporizing the application of the prevailing truth. So *Sanatana* Dharma became Hinduism with a different application. Love and forgiveness was needed in that geographical location at that point in the history of the world. So Christianity was born contemporizing the truth in a method that suited the temperament of people there. Sikhism, Jainism, Buddhism, Islam - the birth of every new religion had only one intent, which is contemporizing the application of the prevailing truth.

Under the current context of lifestyle changes our entertainment is through electricity and artificial lighting. The sunrise and sunset do not impact us as much as it did our ancestors. We live by the watch, by the clock because of artificial lighting. That is why all of us eat when it is lunch time, not because we are hungry; we lie down to sleep at a particular time not because we feel sleepy. Everything is externally triggered and not driven internally.

In this changed lifestyle certain contemporary application has to be evolved. In meditation the attempt is to slow down or quieten your mind. If you have already trained your mind into a dynamic state and then plead that mind to remain quiet - it is not going to happen. This is like you have already made the horse wild, and then asking it to slow down - why will it? So you need to find a time in a day, when your mind is not yet in a dynamic state. Now how do we achieve that?

If you can take a specific time in the day and ensure that you will always begin to withdraw all your senses at that specific time in the day, then over a period of time your system will set itself into this rhythm of gently withdrawing itself and quieten the mind at that time.

Emptier the stomach, greater is the possibility of transcending your mind; the more your stomach is loaded, greater the chances that you will still remain in the thought realm. This is because digestion is one of the most dynamic processes in the human body and as a result the heart beats a lot, a lot of pumping of blood happens, leading to a lot of oxygenation. When there is a lot of oxygen supply to the brain, it always triggers a lot more thoughts, and as a result though you are attempting to transcend the mind you will only have traffic of thoughts.

The key is in choosing a time (when your stomach is empty), a peaceful place to sit in non-doing for meditation and most importantly, consistently practicing meditation during that time of the day in that place daily.

So when the mind is not too dynamic and when the stomach is reasonably empty and if you follow a consistency of time and space, that is, sitting for meditation in a designated place everyday - this will definitely deepen the experience. One day in the balcony, one day in the living room, one day in the pooja room, one day in the bedroom, one day in the terrace will only feed your mind with thoughts. Once you start practicing meditation in a specific place every day, the moment you enter that place, progressively mood will be set for meditation and your mind will get prepared to be quiet. Same time, same place every day; as always, consistency pays rich dividends.

So why do they say you should always meditate in the morning? The chances of you being on an empty stomach and the mind not yet agitated into the corporate demands of your work life is highest during the pre-breakfast time in the morning; so the chances of you slipping very deep into meditation, into a state of non-doing, at that time of the day is very much higher than any other time of the day. ●

*Are there divine preferences, divine injustices and divine irregularities?*

It may appear so, but Existential Order is always zero defect. Everything is as it should be. There are no irregularities in Existence. If I may use a metaphor, it doesn't matter how noble hearted one is, but if the person doesn't know how to drive and yet attempts to drive a vehicle, he or she is sure to meet with an accident. The suffering of most people is that though they may be good, though they may believe in God, they have failed to develop the competence to live life.

We just believe that worshiping god or the messengers of god or the incarnations of god is sufficient to earn His blessing. We are lost in the ignorance that god will come and save us just as an answer to all our pujas, rituals and offerings. We choose to make various kinds of offerings as kickbacks to please the Lord and expedite matters for us, tilt opportunities in our favour, prolong the life of our loved ones, etc... But we have conveniently chosen to ignore principles like Honesty, Integrity, Karma and so many other virtues, which find common mention across all scriptures.

Think about it. If worshiping the Lord is sufficient, then why the Bible? Why the *Quran*? Why the *Bhagavad Gita*? Why any scripture for that matter? In fact, the very basis of every scripture is to teach you and me the components of Existential Order, so that you and I can live our lives in alignment with the Existential Order.

Even if you are a maths teacher's son, if two plus two is written as three, you are wrong. Even if you know nothing about the examiner, if two plus two is written as four, you are right. Even those who do not know 'Who is god?', even those who do not believe in the existence of god, as long as they live in alignment to the Existential Order, which is what every scripture is all about, they will always be blessed by His grace. The more you are aligned to the Existential Order, the more you'll experience His Grace. Grace is the spiritual reward for aligning yourself to the Existential Order. Suffering is a spiritual feedback that somewhere you have lost your alignment to the Existential Order. God is not a matter of belief, but a matter of alignment.

Why did the incarnate Krishna waste his time preaching eighteen chapters, answering and clarifying every question of Arjuna? Krishna could have simply told Arjuna - go around me thrice, pour some milk and ghee over me, smear sandalwood paste all over your body, fall at my feet four times and just shoot your arrows.

Then, why at all the *Bhagavad Gita*? If going to church on Sunday mornings and faith in Christ are enough, then why did Christ waste three years of his life sermonising 'Dos' and 'Don'ts' which became the Bible? If doing *Namaz* five times a day is enough, then why all those 'Dos' and 'Don'ts' in the *Quran*?

The *Mahabharata* shows that *Duryodana* took all the resources of Krishna, and that was not enough. Arjuna had Krishna himself, and that too was not enough. Only when Arjuna understood the Dharma (Existential Order) and acted in alignment with it was he able to emerge victorious. The message is clear and simple - god does not work for you; He works with you. His design is such that the only way He can work with you is when you live in alignment with the Existential Order.

If god is the Messenger, the scriptures are His Message. The only way to have the grace of the Messenger is to live by the Message. It is just not enough to value the Master... you must Master the values. Be devoted to the Messenger, but be disciplined by the Message. •

***The suffering of most people is that though they may be good, though they may believe in God, they have failed to develop the competence to live life.***

mahātria

4

*What is faith?*
*Is faith important*
*to my life?*

The story goes... A man dreamt one night that he was walking along the beach with the Lord. Many scenes from his life flashed across the sky. In each scene he noticed footprints in the sand. Sometimes there were two sets of footprints. Other times there was one set of footprints. This bothered the man because he noticed that during the low periods of his life - when he was suffering from anguish, sorrow, or defeat, he could see only one set of footprints. So he said to the Lord, "You promised me Lord, that if I followed You, You would walk with me always. But I noticed that during the most trying periods of my life there has been only one set of footprints in the sand. Why, when I have needed You the most, You have not been there for me?" The Lord replied, "The times when you have seen only one set of footprints were the times when I carried you." Faith is that trust that He will either walk with you or carry you through.

The seat of your faith is your heart. You are the sole architect of your faith. It is inside out. It is self-authored. Nothing that can enter you through your 5-senses can touch your faith, for your sense organs do not have access to your heart. Faith is beyond sensory perception. It is not a result and effect of data analysis.

Experiences validate faith; they don't cause faith. Faith is not a progression. It is not something you graduate into. It happens in a moment. It is an epiphany. It is a *Satori*. It is a sudden flash of awareness.

Faith is the intelligence of the heart, while belief is the intelligence of the mind. The heart seeks of no proof. The mind is never satisfied with any amount of proof. The heart uses every experience to strengthen the roots of its faith. The mind uses every experience to weaken the very foundation of its belief. Faith grows with time. Beliefs weaken over time. True, not all can have faith in faith. Even truer than that is, none can completely believe his beliefs.

Faith is not anti-science; it is just beyond the comprehension of science. Faith is beyond human judgement. The beginning of every journey, every path, and every voyage, is one of faith - the faith that we will reach, we will arrive, and we will succeed. Faith is the ability to trust what you are not able to see, the ability to believe what is not yet, the ability to 'accept as true' that, which cannot be proven. If faith is believing in what you cannot see, then the reward of faith will be that you will one day see what you always believed in. Faith may be beyond our comprehension, but the results of faith are there for all of us to see.

Once, Hanuman told Rama, "Oh Lord, there is something superior to Thee." Astonished, Rama asked Hanuman, "What is that thing, oh Hanuman, that is superior to me?" Hanuman replied, "Hey Prabho, Thou had crossed the river with the help of a boat. But I crossed the ocean only with the help of the power and strength of Thy Name. The stones floated on the ocean in Thy Name only. Therefore, Thy Name is indeed superior to Thee."

It is not the 'object of faith', but 'faith' that creates miracles. The object of faith is just incidental. It was 'Abba' to Jesus; it was 'Jesus' to Mother Teresa; it was 'Krishna' to Draupadi; it was 'Allah' to Prophet; it was 'Drona' to Ekalavya; it was 'Ram' to Hanuman, and it is 'Hanuman' to many of his devotees. Yet, all of them have experienced the miraculous power of faith in their lives, which confirms that it is not the 'object of faith', but it is the 'faith in the object' that creates miracles.

Faith transforms an ordinary vibration of thought, created by the finite mind of an individual, into a spiritual equivalent. Faith is the only gate through which the cosmic force of Infinite Intelligence can be harnessed and used by everyone. Like ideas, which are more powerful than the mind that gave birth to them, faith too is more potent than the 'object' on which the faith is directed.

However, human beings made a great error of judgement. Whenever they experienced the miraculous happenings that faith unfolded, they credited the results to their 'object of faith', not realising that it was their 'faith in the object' that was unfolding those miracles. Due to this error of judgement, they did everything from rituals, offerings and sacrifices to please their 'object of faith'. They even changed their 'object of faith' periodically; from one form of God to another... they focused on everything but their very faith. It isn't a question of how powerful your 'God' is... it's a question of how powerful is your 'faith' in God.

The power of the object of your faith is derived from the power of your faith in the object.

A classic metaphor for faith is the little child who holds the finger of his parent to cross the road, and just moves along with the finger - stepping forward sometimes, running sometimes, pausing sometimes, stepping backward sometimes - but eventually crosses the road, still holding on to the finger. In faith, everything works. Without faith, nothing works. With no faith, you will know fear. When you know faith, there will be no fear. Faith and fear cannot coexist, like the profound English proverb iterates, "Fear knocked at the door and faith answered, 'No one here'." Let faith in and fear will get out.

Choices are born out of human intelligence and consequences are born out of His intelligence. Faith is in knowing that His intelligence will prevail, always. Faith is in knowing that sometimes your plans will be upset, so that He can execute His plans for you, and His plans are always right for you. That's why, in faith you don't ask, "Why is this happening to me?" But you do ask with faith, "By putting me through all this, what are you preparing me for, my Lord? What is the bigger picture my Lord, that I am not able to see yet?" The force that brings you to it will also bring you through it.

While sorrow looks back and worry looks around, faith looks up. Faith is the basis of your relationship with the force above... the force beyond... the force within.

Like the little ones, with faith, take the plunge... into a future that's awaiting you. ●

5

*You keep quoting from all religions. Which religion do you belong to?*

If I put these words on one side - *aum, amen, namaz, micchami dukkadam, kirpan,* and write the names of some religions on the other side, Sikhism, Islam, Hinduism, Christianity and Jainism, you will be able to match each word to a specific religion.

Now let me quote few other words... god, love, humanity, gratitude, prayer, peace, bliss, silence, forgiveness, abundance, nature, life and death... which specific religion will you associate these words with?

In the entirety of the Universe, which is made up of millions of galaxies, our galaxy (Milky Way) is just a speck of dust. In Milky Way, which is made up of millions of solar systems, our solar system (with sun in the middle) is just a speck of dust. In our solar system, which is made up of innumerable celestial bodies, our planet (Earth) is just a speck of dust. In our planet, which is made up of countless animate and inanimate forms, humanity is just a speck of dust.

Except this speck of dust - humanity, everything else is able to function zero-defect without having to identify with any specific religion.

I, the dustest of all dusts (English doesn't have a word to describe how insignificant I feel when I consider the limitlessness of this Existence), just want to remain the child of god, who will agree with me, He too does not belong to any religion. I, as His child, follow all religions but do not belong to any religion.

True spiritual evolution is to transcend the bondages of all religions. No religion can own me and I own no religion. ●

***God, love, humanity, gratitude,***
***prayer, peace, bliss, silence,***
***forgiveness, abundance,***
***nature, life and death...***
***which specific religion***
***will you associate these words with?***

***Except this speck of dust - humanity,***
***everything else is able to***
***function zero-defect***
***without having to identify***
***with any specific religion.***

# 6

*Whenever I am going through a purple patch in life, I know my energy is right, and it's manifesting itself in all the dimensions. When I am going through failure, somewhere my energy is not right; so how do I get my energy right?*

Let us first understand something about ourselves first. All human beings have three major dimensions in their personality; they are physical, psychological and spiritual. The physical dimension is the form of a person, something that all of us can see. The psychological dimension is the thoughts and feelings of a person. The spiritual dimension is the energy that manifests through the thoughts and feelings of a person which culminates in an action in the physical dimension.

For example, when we switch on an electric bulb, it should emit light. On switching it on, if the bulb does not emit light, the first thing that we would check is, if the fuse is intact or not. That is the physical level. Now if the bulb looks alright with its fuse in place, then we would check the wiring for cuts or damages. That is the psychological level. Now if the bulb is alright and the wiring is also alright and still if the bulb is not burning, then there may not be right power supply to the wire. That is the spiritual level or the energy level.

When power supply is not there, even if everything else, the bulb and the wire is alright, the bulb will not burn and emit light, isn't it? In the same way when the right energy is not there, even if the physical and psychological dimensions are working fine, things may not go right in one's life.

Energy has no character by itself; depending on which medium it manifests it becomes heat energy or nuclear energy or any other form of energy. That is, depending on the medium it manifests, it takes a different character.

Haven't you noticed that when you are in the presence of some people, you feel so peaceful and in the presence of some others you feel so very agitated, for no reason at all. This is because when you are present with an another being, you exchange energy with the other, all the time; so due to this exchange of energy you are either positively charged or contaminated by the other.

So, we have to get our life at the spiritual level right by getting the energy right. How can we get the energy level right?

Already a prescription has been given to us many years ago by Buddha.

*Buddham Charanam Gacchami; Dhammam Charanam Gacchami; Sangam Charanam Gacchami.*

*Buddham Charanam Gacchami:* That is the first option he gives. If you want to get your life right in all the three dimensions, the spiritual, psychological and the physical level, you need to share a dynamic relationship with a spiritually evolved soul or you need to be physically in a place which is high on energy levels, vibrations.

Traditionally, whenever enlightened people discovered a place with high vibrations, they initiated a place of worship in that location. The science behind places of worship is to create a space where people can come and inherit the vibrations of that place. When a person stands inside a rose garden long enough, won't he or she come out smelling roses?

The energy of existence that runs this entire cosmos, has chosen to flow through a few spiritually evolved souls; they have found a way to merge into this universal source of energy and that energy is expressing through them.

By sitting in a state of non-doing, either in a space of high vibrations or in the presence of a spiritually evolved soul who carries high vibrations, the vibrations will be transferred unto you. And in the presence of higher vibrations, everything will go right. You will go through a purple patch.

But Buddha was a very practical man, so he realized that it is not possible for everybody to find a Buddha in their lives. So, Buddha gave you a second option...

*Dhammam Charanam Gacchami:* If you cannot be with the teacher (Buddha), all the time, be with the teachings of the teacher (*Dhammam*). Even if you cannot be with the messenger all the time, be with the message all the time.

The energy of a teacher is present in his teachings. That is why even after thousands of years, the *Bhagavad Gita* or the *Quran* or the Bible or the Jain Dharma, or the *Dhammapada* is still relevant to everybody's life. It never becomes outdated because they don't carry printed words; they carry the energy of the Master filled in it.

So, when you read and internalize the message of the messenger two things happen; one, message gets your psychological personality right and two, the energy of the messenger in the message gets your spiritual personality right.

Buddha's third option is, *Sangam Charanam Gacchami.*

All of us strive to become better than what we are presently, and we need help for that. We need the right environment for that. So, Buddha said *Sangam Charanam Gacchami* meaning surround yourself with like-minded people. My addition to it will be like-minded and most importantly, right-minded people.

A research was done by Kellogg Business School on their alumni and they found that the net worth of every individual is the average of the 10 people they relate most with. The truth is our environment passes on its character to us. So, choose your environment, choose the company of right-minded people and shun wrong-minded people to get your life right. Need be walk alone...

Essentially to get your energy level right, *Buddham Charanam Gacchami; Dhammam Charanam Gacchami; Sangam Charanam Gacchami.* The purple patch will return to your life... ●

7

*Why people offer their hair to God?*

One interpretation is that hair is a significant element in one's looks. Hair is a matter of pride for men and women alike. In offering your hair to God, you are, in the spiritual sense, offering your pride and ego to God.

Another interpretation to it is in the days of monarchy, at the end of a battle, the defeated king would place his crown at the feet of the victorious king, symbolising surrender. Here surrender has a different connotation. It doesn't mean defeat. Here surrender means, 'Till now I was responsible for the welfare of my subjects. Now that my kingdom has become your kingdom, I surrender the welfare of my people in your hands. Take care of them'. Here surrender means 'transference of responsibility'. By offering the crown, the defeated king had transferred the responsibility of the welfare of his people to the victorious king. For us, the common people, hair is our crown. By offering our hair to the lord, you are basically stating, 'I place my sense of pride at your feet. I surrender myself unto you my lord. I am transferring the responsibility of my life in Thee hands. Lead me through'.

So it is with life. By surrender you are just making God a major partner in your endeavours. Not everything in life happens the way we want it to happen. We are too immature to understand the larger picture. In not understanding the larger picture, we let the temporary speed breakers and transitory hurdles that we face in life to disturb us. Surrender helps us to understand that 'We may be tested, but never forsaken'. Sometimes God does upset our plans so that He can execute His plans for us. His plans are always right for us. We can go through these challenges in a state of total peace only through surrender. By surrendering yourself to that infinite intelligence, you are allowing that infinite intelligence to express itself through you.

If your surrender is total, surrender always works. In fact, nothing works like surrender. But many people neither trust their own surrender, nor do they trust the object of their surrender. Surrender, if it lacks trust then it is not surrender at all.

Ego is 'Everything of me and Nothing of you'. Surrender is 'Nothing of me and Everything of you'. In surrender, you are left with only one question: 'What are you preparing me for, my Lord?' Surrender is an expression of total trust. ●

***Ego is***
***'Everything of me***
***and***
***Nothing of you'.***

***Surrender is***
***'Nothing of me***
***and***
***Everything of you'.***

8

*Sometimes, being very far away from my Guru I still feel I am right next to him. Is it my imagination or does vibrations need no time and space. Please explain.*

A Guru is a presence and not a person. And, a presence is beyond time and space. So, where is the question of being 'far away from my Guru'? The very phrase doesn't fit into a seeker's relationship with the Guru. Distance and time are associated only with something outside of you. But, a Guru is a presence in you; with you; operating from within you... the intelligence behind your intelligence; the energy of your life; your very subconscious; in fact, your DNA. As much as you cannot be away from yourself, after even a simple glimpse of oneness with a Guru, you can no more be away from that presence.

There is no time and space, not only in the world of vibrations, but also in a relationship between the seeker and the Guru. It is a relationship of deep love, reverence, surrender, and faith. It is a presence with inexplicable gravitation. There is a constant pull... a lingering presence that transforms the very chemistry of your being.

The closer you feel with your Guru, the closer you feel with yourself. The more you are attracted towards the Guru, the more independent you become. The more surrendered you feel to the Guru, the more you feel your own freedom.

Though there is air everywhere within your body and around your body, breathing is concentrated through the nostrils. Similarly, though divinity is omnipresent and vibrations are omniscient, the concentrated source to experience it is the Guru. That's why, if you have found such a presence with which you are able to experience oneness, then there can be no greater blessing than this.

The *Upanishads* state, in the presence of the *Satguru*, knowledge flourishes, sorrow diminishes, joy wells up without any reason, abundance dawns, and all talents manifest.

However, I can understand your confusion. A seeker's relationship with the Guru does begin with the person; begins with communication; begins through the senses; begins with doubt; begins like any other relationship; begins as an outside-in experience. However, the more and more you grow in love with your Guru, the more and more you are able to understand the love of your Guru, it becomes a presence; it becomes a communion; it transcends the senses; it becomes one of faith; it becomes a oneness like no other relationship; it becomes inside-out.

Entering a rose garden, staying in the rose garden and feeling one with the rose garden are all the physical side of the experience. There is a spiritual side to this experience. A moment comes when you too start smelling like the roses. The fragrance of the garden has become your fragrance. Now, much after you leave the garden (far away from your Guru), you will still feel the fragrance in you (you still feel you are right next to him).

The only befitting expression of a seeker is, "Guru, when I am with you, I am with you. Even when I am not with you, I am still with you. There are times when I am not there. Even then, you are always there."

The only befitting expression of a Guru is, "My beloved, you are no more alone. I am with you always." ●

***The only befitting expression***
***of a seeker is,***
***"Guru, when I am with you,***
***I am with you.***
***Even when I am not with you,***
***I am still with you."***

mahātria

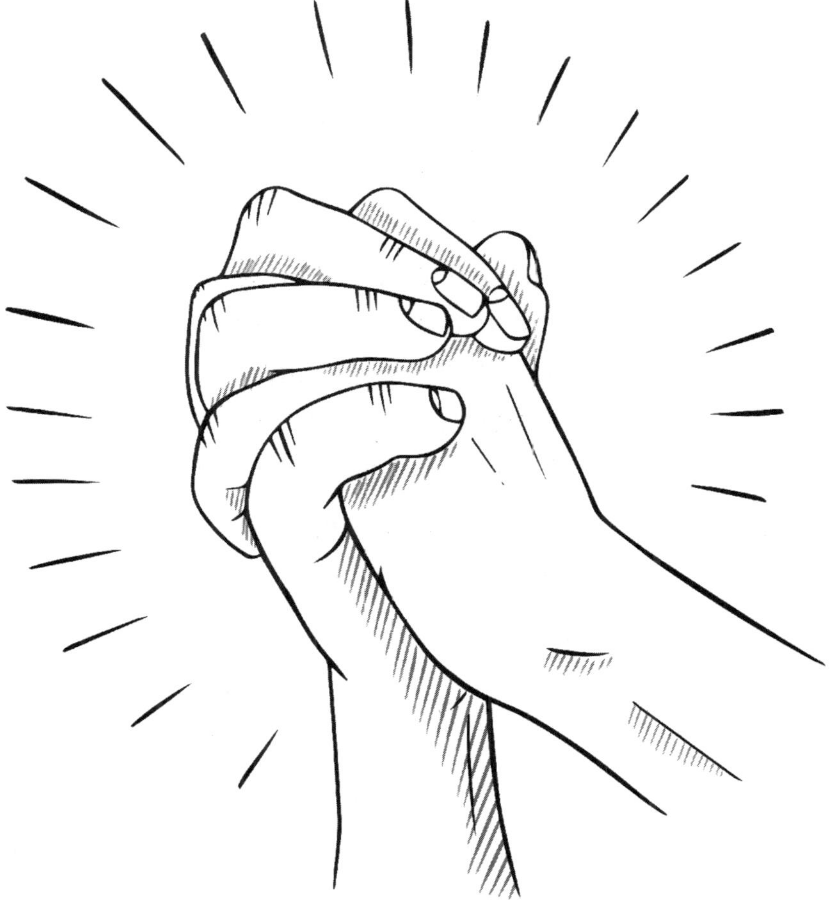

9

*You keep stating,*
*"True spiritual evolution*
*is to outgrow the bondage*
*of all religions." But,*
*is it practical for someone*
*to have grown in one faith*
*to be able to accept*
*another faith?*

In fact, "True spiritual evolution is to outgrow all discriminations," and one of those is the bondage of religion. Every act of discrimination, every thought of discrimination - whether in the name of religion or sex or language or for whatever, is self-imprisonment. Intents of discrimination affect the very flow and rhythm of life. It makes you run after some, and run away from some; but in truth, life cannot be segmented. Life is whole and it has to be lived holistically. And, holistic life is experienced only when you outgrow discrimination.

Rabindranath Tagore said, "Where the world has not been broken up into fragments by narrow domestic walls... into that heaven of freedom Father, let my country awake."

Sri Ramakrishna Paramahamsa said, "All religions are true. God can be reached by different religions. Many rivers flow by many ways, but they fall into the sea. They all are one. Every man should follow his own religion. A Christian should follow Christianity, and a Mohammedan, Mohammedanism. For the Hindu, the ancient path, the path of the Aryan *Rishis*, is the best."

In *Bhagavad-Gita*, Chapter 18, in the verses 64 to 66, Lord Krishna states,

- Again hear My most confidential of all paramount instructions; being very dear to Me, I am speaking for your benefit.

- Just think of Me, be My devotee, worship Me, offer obeisance unto Me, certainly you will come to Me, I promise this in truth to you being dear to Me.

- Relinquishing all ideas of righteousness, surrender unto Me exclusively; I will deliver you from all sinful reactions, do not despair.

And, if we are objective enough, the 'Me' can represent Krishna or you can replace the 'Me' with Rama or Shiva or Buddha, or Jesus, and the verses will still hold true. These verses aren't about the 'Me' - that's Him, but about you and the transformation that's required of you to reach Him.

As an IT professional, which of the following companies will you refuse to work, if you get a breakthrough? Wipro, Infosys or TCS? So does it make a difference that Azim Premji is a Muslim by birth; Narayana Murthy is a Hindu by birth; Ratan Tata is a Parsee by birth?

Your source of money has no religion. Your source of food has no religion. The doctors and nurses who save your life are seen beyond religion. Our academic knowledge has come from sources that are beyond religion. The soldiers work together to protect a nation beyond their individualistic religious backgrounds. Irrespective of their religious backgrounds, we soulfully enjoy the music of A R Rahman, Illaiyaraja, Harris Jayaraj and Daler Mehndi. Why then, when it comes to understanding the philosophies of life alone, should we close our minds to the infinite wisdom that's available?

When management ideas can come from Tom Peters and the secret of health can be learnt from Deepak Chopra, why not open our minds to the philosophies of life from all and any faith?

I don't have to answer your question. In fact, a hymn from Rig Veda (1.89.1) states, “Let noble thoughts come to us from all sides.”

Leave the religious backgrounds and the sentiments associated to it. Purely from an intellectual perspective, let us see what Jesus has to say on life, and examine if it applies to us, irrespective of our religious backgrounds.

Matthew 7:12 states, “So in everything, do to others what you would have them do to you, for this sums up the Law and the Prophets.”

To overcome double standards in relationships, to be empathetic in relationships, to be able to sensitise ourselves with others' feelings, to know what it feels from the other's shoes, to operate out of 'You Win - I Win' frame of mind, to be fair-minded in dealing with people - for all that to be achieved in relationships, simply, do to others what you would have them do to you.

Psalm 46:10 states, "Be still, and know that I am God."

Even if the Petronas Twin Towers are thrown in the Pacific Ocean, it won't create ripples. Just a small pebble in a still water lake will create endless ripples. If you will have to listen to Him, the noise within you has to stop.

About maintaining stillness, Franz Kafka beautifully wrote, "You do not need to leave your room. Remain sitting at your table and listen. Do not even listen, simply wait, be quiet, still and solitary. The world will freely offer itself to you to be unmasked, it has no choice, it will roll in ecstasy at your feet." Peak dynamic state is achieved from peak static state. The power of doing is derived from experiencing the power of non-doing. Practice stillness to gain materialistically and also to grow spiritually.

Matthew 18:21-22 states: Peter asked, "Lord, how often should I forgive someone who sins against me? Seven times?" Jesus replied, "No! Seventy times seven!" In Mark 11:25-26, Jesus said, "But when you are praying, first forgive anyone you are holding a grudge against, so that your Father in heaven will forgive your sins, too." And finally, in Luke 23:34, "Father forgive them, for they know not what they do."

In all, forgiveness has been the central theme. Between the hater and the hated, it is always the hater who gets hurt more. So, for your own peace, forgive others. Forgiveness is not liberating the other from you but liberating yourself from the other. So, for your own liberation, release the person who is sitting in your heart and mind and disturbing your peace by forgiving him. Only through forgiveness, you can release your emotional baggage. Else, you keep building them.

Luke 6:27-29 states, "But I tell you who hear me: Love your enemies; do good to those who hate you; bless those who curse you; pray for those who mistreat you. If someone strikes you on one cheek, turn to him the other also."

Mahatma Gandhi, considered the Father of this Nation, for having led the Indian freedom movement, just epitomised this. Simply put, others being bad can't be an excuse for you to be bad. It needs enormous character strength to choose to be good, even to those who have not been good to you.

In Matthew 17:20 it is stated, Jesus said, "I tell you the truth, if you have faith as small as a mustard seed, you can say to this mountain, 'Move from here to there' and it will move. Nothing will be impossible for you."

Faith works. Faith alone works. With his faith in Rama, Hanuman was able to fly across the ocean, though, for Rama the bridge had to be made. True, faith can move mountains.

In John 8:7, Jesus said, "If any one of you is without sin, let him be the first to throw a stone at her."

Let's focus on getting ourselves right than finding out where others are wrong. Let's not expect perfection from the world without us being perfect ourselves. Let's not cut other's leg for us to look tall. By proving others wrong we don't make our life right. Let's not speak ill of others - we derive nothing from it. Let's use our intelligence to get ourselves right than using it to find out where others are wrong. ●

***Peak dynamic state***
***is achieved from***
***peak static state.***
***The power of doing***
***is derived from experiencing***
***the power of non-doing.***

mahātria

10

*So many religions claim that it is the only holy revelation. All the religions do differ in some aspects. What is the true guidance?*

Religion, in its innate sense has been purely sentimental and has not been accepted by the world as an intellectual path. I think, religion, cult, fraternity, forum, society, *samaj*, different names we give to a group of people who follow a common doctrine. So in a way everything is religion; in a way nothing is religion. In essence what is religion? That which takes you back to your origin is religion.

The word religion has its Latin roots: *Re Ligare*, that is, *Re* (again) *Ligare* (to reconnect). Two essential understandings: One, the purpose of religion is to help me to again reconnect to my origin, which is unison. Two, only when a path helps me to achieve unison it has served its purpose as a religion. What's your origin? You emerged in the fusion between the formless and the form. And from there you came in. So if you can be taken to a point of meditative silence, if you can be taken to a point where you are able to dissolve into your creator, if you are ever able to be taken to a point where you are no more able to separate yourself from that existential presence, whichever path has done this to you, whether you call it as a religion or not, is a religion. Religion is not necessarily Hinduism, Jainism, Sikhism, Christianity, Islam.

Most terrorist activities are manifestations of religious fanaticism. We may not be a direct sponsor to these terrorist activities but most of us are religious fanatics. Most people are social hypocrites. Even the most intelligent of men become utterly foolish when it comes to their religious sentiments. Each and every one of us should cry in shame for the way we have abused the wisdom of our spiritual masters.

Can't we embrace God without embracing religious fanaticism? Can't we experience God without a chosen classified place of worship? Can't we have an identity of our own than the one borrowed from religion? Can't we be good and noble human beings and avoid religious bloodshed? Can't we embrace humanity with a sense of equality dropping behind all religion-based inequality? Can't we make a beginning in our own way?

Religious tolerance alone will not be enough. We must renounce religious fanaticism. Will God reject us if we go to Him as a human being, just plain simple human being, without any religious prefixes or suffixes? I claimed that I am from this religion because my dad said that he was from this religion. I simply wish to remain as a child of God, for I believe that, like me, God transcends any particular religious affiliation. In my view, neither God nor I can be confined within the boundaries of a single religion.

Let us walk our life with purity of thoughts towards spiritual evolution. ●

***The purpose of religion***
***is to help me***
***to again reconnect to my origin,***
***which is Unison.***

mahātria

11

*Whenever I don't think much about something it happens to me. Whereas, when I think and plan it falls apart. So is it better to just 'go with the flow' and not think about things at all?*

'Flowing with the flow' is one of the highest attributes of spiritual alignment. So, never block the flow. But remember, faith does not free a person of his or her responsibilities. There is enough and more for all of us in this world but we got to think, plan and execute in order to have it. The issue is not with thinking and planning. Like how a little poison is enough to contaminate a pond of potable water, even a little doubt is enough to neutralise faith. Also, whenever the subconscious is given mixed associations, it does not play its part in progress. For example, I hope in becoming rich I don't lose out on my personal life. I feel very close to him but I live in this constant fear that one day I might lose him. Such patterns in thoughts cause things to fall apart. Never create mixed associations of positive and negative and thus incapacitate your subconscious.

If there is a pattern in your life, like what you mentioned above, then there is a pattern to your thoughts. Get the thinking patterns right, and you will get your life right. ●

12

*The concept of 'Unison' assumes I am different from GOD and pre-supposes duality. But GOD and I are always ONE and there is therefore no Unison. Is my understanding right?*

Absolutely true! Intellectually, absolutely true! As a matter of truth, absolutely true! The effect is nothing but the cause itself in a different form. Every creation is creator embedded. There is no question about it. But, the very fact you do not have an experience of it, but only an intellectual understanding of the same, you keep seeking.

If God and you are always one, then why do you pray? Then, who is praying to whom? If God and you are always one, then there is no space and time that divides God and you. Then, why go to a place of worship? Then, who is worshipping whom? If God and you are one, then why are you asking this very question to another human being? Why does God want clarity from another human being?

In all this, your ego is very much present, which is not giving you the experience of that Unison, that oneness with God. Duality doesn't exist in reality but your ego causes the perception of duality. It is by transcending your identification with your mind, intellect and emotions, you will annihilate your ego, and thus transcend the perceptional duality, and for the first time experientially experience that God and you are always one, the state of Unison. And, only after that, this question will dissolve from your mind. Till then, all these concepts, which you are intellectually aware of, will purely serve argumentative questioning and debates. For you, there is no experiential validation, yet. Seek to dissolve your ego, which is causing this duality, and for the first time you will experientially understand *Advaita*. Knowing is nothing. Experience is everything. ●